SEVEN DEADLY SINS, SEVEN LIVELY VIRTUES

STUDY GUIDE

A Catholic Study Program presented by
BISHOP ROBERT BARRON

Study Guide written by
BISHOP ROBERT BARRON
&
MARK P. SHEA

✝ THIRD EDITION ✝

www.WORDONFIRE.org
© 2018 Word on Fire Catholic Ministries

SEVEN DEADLY SINS, SEVEN LIVELY VIRTUES

TABLE OF CONTENTS

Introduction:	A Deeper Look at Sin & Virtue	1
Lesson I:	Pride & Humility	9
Lesson II:	Envy & Admiration	17
Lesson III:	Anger & Forgiveness	25
Lesson IV:	Sloth & Zeal	33
Lesson V:	Avarice & Generosity	41
Lesson VI:	Gluttony & Asceticism	49
Lesson VII:	Lust & Chastity	57

BIOGRAPHICAL INFORMATION   67
    Bishop Robert Barron
    Mark P. Shea

INTRODUCTION

Welcome to Bishop Robert Barron's enlightening study on sin and virtue. Over the course of this study, we will look at what Catholic tradition calls the Seven Deadly Sins and contrast them with what Bishop Barron refers to as the Seven Lively Virtues. This study guide is designed to help you understand and apply what you learn from Bishop Barron's video talks about these seven sins.

The Study Guide's aim is to increase understanding, promote reflection, and encourage practical action. You will have the chance to dig into the Catholic tradition and grapple with Scripture and the Church's teaching as it is summarized in the *Catechism of the Catholic Church (CCC)*. You will also be able to use this study to assess and enhance your life as a disciple of Jesus Christ. The guide is built around QUESTIONS FOR UNDERSTANDING and QUESTIONS FOR APPLICATION, which will reinforce the main points made in each section on a Deadly Sin and its corresponding Lively Virtue. Throughout the study, you will be asked to look up different Bible verses and passages from the *Catechism of the Catholic Church (CCC)*.

In the introductory video, Bishop Barron presents a framework for understanding what sin is and why it happens. He begins by saying, "God does not need you. You have been loved into existence and that is where your worth comes from." In response to this generous gift of love, we should all relax and allow the love of God to surge through us to others. God's economy is different than the world's—the more you give God's love away, the more you get. The more you give God's gifts away, the more you get. But we don't know this because we have forgotten who we are, and how we came into existence through God's love.

Not knowing our true worth, we become afraid and start to justify ourselves and try to prove that we have value. Many believe that if they get enough wealth, material things, pleasure, power or honor, they'll be worth something. This attitude does not allow you to give away God's gifts; it promotes grasping those gifts and keeping them to oneself, fearful that others might take them away. Spiritual masters describe this state of fear as being "caved in on oneself"

or being tied up in negative attitudes and distortions of the spirit that lead to sin. This self-imposed imprisonment keeps us from being fully alive as God wants us to be. This attitude is deadly, and the most egregious symptoms of this imprisonment can be called the "deadly sins."

The great Italian Catholic poet, Dante Alighieri, wrote about these sins in *Purgatorio*, the second part of his masterpiece, *The Divine Comedy.* This epic poem opens in the year 1300, when its protagonist was 35, mid-life by a Biblical reckoning: "The measure of our life is seventy years…" (Ps. 90:10). As psychologists and spiritual teachers over the centuries have testified, mid-life is often a time of crisis and breakthrough. The justly celebrated opening lines of the *Comedy* signal this truth: "Midway on the journey of our life, I woke to find myself alone in a dark wood, having wandered from the straight path." Though he was a massively accomplished man, renowned in both the artistic and political arenas, Dante was, by his mid-thirties, spiritually lost. That he realized this—that he woke up to it, to use his metaphor—was a blessing and the impetus for his journey, much as "hitting bottom" and "turning one's life over to a higher power" are essential for those undertake a Twelve-Step process.

He meets the ghost of the Roman poet Virgil, who functions as his spiritual director and guide. Virgil tells the troubled Dante that there is a way forward but that it involves a journey through Hell. In our "I'm okay and you're okay" culture, this is a very difficult message to take in, but every authentic spiritual master acknowledges its indispensability. We have to confront our sin and dysfunction with complete honesty; otherwise we will get stuck. So, Virgil first leads Dante on a tour of the underworld.

After having gone all the way down to Hell, Dante is now ready to rise. Moving through the center of the earth, he comes out the other side and commences a journey up Mount Purgatory. On each level of that seven-story mountain, one of the deadly sins—pride, envy, anger, sloth, avarice, gluttony, and lust—is punished, usually through some version of moving in the direction opposite of one's sin. Bishop Barron sees these countervailing actions for sin as the Seven Lively Virtues. Each virtue is an antidote, meant to be practiced in order to turn from that particular sinful pattern.

At the top of mountain, Dante has been cleansed of all sin and freed from the burden and heaviness of sin, so he is light enough to fly to Paradise. He commences a flight through the various levels of heaven. What he sees are, in essence, different dimensions of love, for heaven *is* nothing but love. Finally, at the very end of his pilgrimage, the poet is permitted to look into the face of God, which he appreciates as "the love that moves the Sun and the other stars."

QUESTIONS FOR UNDERSTANDING

1. Read the *Catechism of the Catholic Church* (CCC) paragraphs 1849-1851 and 1866. What is sin? What are the Seven Deadly Sins?

2. Read CCC 1803 and Philippians 4:8. What is virtue? Why is it important in the spiritual life?

   The God of Peace will be with you, honorable lovely gracious

3. Read Wisdom 1. What are the qualities of wisdom? What are the qualities of the wise or righteous person? What are the qualities of the unwise fool?

4. Read CCC 759. As a sheer, gratuitous gift, God intends that you exist and share in his divine life. What response does this require from us?

Love

QUESTIONS FOR APPLICATION

1. The startling proposition, "God does not need you" affects different people in different ways. Some people might feel relief. Others might feel resentment. Still others might feel puzzlement. What is your response to that proposition?

2. St. Thomas Aquinas says that love is "willing the good of the other as other." Can you think of examples of this that you have witnessed either in your own life or in the lives of others? Can you describe an experience of having been a conduit for God's love?

3. Bishop Barron also warns of the opposite danger of a "love" that is really "indirect egotism." Can you think of times in your life when you have "loved" somebody in order to get him/her to do something for you and not because you actually cared about his/her good? Or, how about a time when your relationship with a person took precedence over your relationship with God? How did you recognize and overcome temptations like this?

4. Bishop Barron describes fear as being at the root of all sin. Have you ever experienced fear working against the virtue of love in your life? How can fear lead you to forget the love of God and put your trust somewhere else?

5. What makes sin deadly? How can God's anger be good news for us? Have you ever experienced sin's killing effect? Have you ever seen God's liberation from that deadliness at work in your life? What was that like?

NOTES:

PRIDE & HUMILITY

The souls on Mount Purgatory in Dante's *Divine Comedy* do various forms of penance for their sins in ways that reflect both the nature of their sins and the way to salvation from those sins. Pride is at the base of the mountain, the heaviest place, because pride is the deadliest of the deadly sins. In fact, all sin is in some way a form of pride because sin elevates our ego ahead of all other concerns.

From a theological perspective, pride makes you into God. Pride causes you to assume the prerogatives and centrality of God, to make your own self the center of the world. One example of this attitude of playing God can be seen in a line from the Supreme Court decision, *Planned Parenthood vs. Casey:* "At the heart of liberty, is the right to define one's own concept of existence, of meaning, of the universe, and the mystery of human life." This attitude equates individual freedom with the capacity to determine good and evil, and be the supreme power over one's own existence.

Pride, in the spiritual sense, keeps us wrapped up in our own little adventures and projects, which ultimately cause boredom and sadness. In contrast, God's way opens us up to adventures bigger than we could ever dream of ourselves. His way is expansive, beyond the small confines of our own ego. In our fallen world, we forget so readily that we are only creatures; we come to expect that things are owed to us and start to think of ourselves as gods.

Dante's punishment for the proud is that they bear heavy boulders on their backs that weigh them down, as if they were carrying an ego-monkey around that needed to be attended to constantly. The boulders also force them to bend down and look at the reality of the earth from which they came. This reveals the quintessential truth about life: we are creatures "of the earth" and not the creators of good and evil, right and wrong. Simply stated, God is God and we are not.

The antidote to pride is humility. To learn humility is to learn to live in the reality that each of us is a creature of God, worshipping him and surrendering to him and to his plans for us. If humble, you can live lightly and freely because you no longer carry the great ego-boulder around. To believe in God is to know the truth; to live out of that truth is to live in the attitude

of humility. Living out the deepest truth of things puts us as creatures in right relationship with God, the creator.

Bishop Barron offers some practical advice to combat pride:

- Purposely take the lower place at gatherings
- Consciously opt out of the ego game, refusing to scramble for honor and status
- Learn to love simple things in the way that children do
- Model the Blessed Mother's attitude at the Annunciation, "Be it done to me according to your word," and the great adventure of God's mission for you will begin.

QUESTIONS FOR UNDERSTANDING

1. Read Matthew 5:3, 2 Corinthians 8:9, Proverbs 16:18-19 and CCC 2546. What does it mean to be "poor in spirit"? How does this attitude contrast with pride? How does Jesus model this? How can we imitate that in practical ways?

2. Read CCC 2547. Can the proud truly abandon themselves to "the providence of the Father"? Why or why not?

3. Read CCC 2631. How can pride stand in the way of forgiveness, prayer, and right worship?

4. Read Philippians 2:1-11. What qualities does Paul encourage us to have? How does he base this command on Jesus Christ? What did Jesus do, according to Paul?

5. Read Luke 1:46-55. How does Mary model humility? What are some of the things Mary says that our culture does not tend to identify as "humble" statements? How does this illuminate the differences between the biblical understanding of humility and our cultural notions of it?

QUESTIONS FOR APPLICATION

1. Bishop Barron mentions the famous "mystery clause" from the Supreme Court's "Casey vs. Planned Parenthood Decision," which declares: "At the heart of liberty is the right to define one's own concept of existence, of meaning, of the universe, and of the mystery of human life." How does this understanding of freedom differ from a Christian understanding? What are some of the consequences of this understanding of freedom?

2. Dante puts pride at the bottom of Mount Purgatory as the heaviest and deadliest sin to be purged. Have you ever thought of pride as the worst sin, or do you tend to think other sins are worse? Why is pride the worst sin? How have you seen pride at work in your life?

3. Dante represents the penance for pride as carrying heavy boulders on the back. Have you had to suffer for pride? What was it like? Has God brought healing out of that suffering? What was that like?

4. Humility is described variously as being "earthy," or living in truth, or being self-forgetful. How and when have you experienced these things? Have you ever known a humble person? What was he or she like?

5. A good first step toward cultivating the virtue of humility is to purposely take the lower place and not merely the equal place to somebody else. Aristotle uses the image of bending the stick backward, not merely bending it straight. Have you ever put yourself lower than a competitor? Is there somebody in your life to whom you need to cede the higher place? What concrete step could you take to do that?

NOTES:

ENVY & ADMIRATION

As we continue climbing Mount Purgatory, we come to the second level, where Envy is purged. Envy is pleasure in the sorrow of another or resentment over their happiness or success. St. Thomas Aquinas called envy "irrational anger at the success of others" and "sorrow at another person's good." Both Scripture and the great literature of the world often speak to us of the deadly effects of envy. Think of the Biblical stories: Cain slays Able out of jealousy; Jacob tricks his father to get Esau's birthright; Saul is envious of David and wants to kill him. Anyone who sees or reads even a few Shakespeare plays sees envy and jealousy taking center stage often.

Envy is the daughter of pride because it involves comparing others to yourself and believing that you should have or be what the other has or is. Gore Vidal, a fiction writer from the late 20th century, put it bluntly when he said, "When a friend of mine succeeds, something in me dies." Something in us dies and we often want to go after that person who stirs envy within us. So, scapegoating often occurs as we try to tear down the other person.

Envy is, like all the deadly sins, a "capital" or "head" sin because it is a fountain from which other evil acts flow, such as theft, betrayal, and even murder. Ambition is closely tied to envy and often driven by it. Advising early Christians in Jerusalem (and contemporary Christians as well), St. James writes: "Where jealousy and selfish ambition exist, there is disorder and every foul practice" (James 3:16). When you are seized by envy or ambition, your whole life will be overcome by them and all your actions will be directed by their power.

As fear is the root of all sin, envy comes from the fear that "I'm not as valuable or important as someone else." This attitude symbolizes a battle within oneself which, if left unchecked, gives rise to external conflicts:

> "Where do the wars and where do the conflicts among you come from? Is it not from your passions that make war within your members? You covert but do not possess. You kill and envy but you cannot obtain; you fight and wage war. You do not possess because you do not ask. You ask but you do not receive, because you ask wrongly, to spend it on your passions." -James 4:1-3

When we are centered in envy or ambition and not in Christ, who keeps all parts of our life in balance, an interior jumble ensues. When you fall apart on the inside, you usually cause trouble on the outside. Envy can, very directly, cause much damage and evil. The envious don't realize or understand the deepest truth — God is loving them into existence *always*. We are all connected in a body of people being loved by God. We all have gifts, but they are not all the same as each of us has a different mission from the Lord. It is not a zero-sum game if we realize that we are all being loved and blessed by God; you succeed, I succeed, you suffer, I suffer. Our true happiness is found by joining our lives in love with God and others, who also have been loved into being by God.

As punishment (and medicine), the eyes of the envious are sewn shut in Dante's *Paradisio*. Since the envious spend their lives looking at others, this penance stops them from seeing at all, so they cannot resent the success of others.

The lively virtue for envy is admiration for all the gifts God has bestowed on each person. God is the source of all existence and "all is gift," even our intelligence, will, and capacity. Acknowledging and admiring God's gifts in others, while accepting that everything comes from God, we can profess with Isaiah: "Lord, you have accomplished all we have done" (Isa 26:12). Envy flows from forgetting this basic truth.

Bishop Barron offers practical advice to thwart envy, which is to go out of your way to praise whomever you envy. If you are in a group that is scapegoating someone, purposely put a wrench in the discussion by interrupting it with praise for the scapegoat. Realize that the dispensing of different gifts is linked to different missions from the Lord, but all are in one Body of Christ. Concentrate on your unique role in this mystical Body and stop comparing yourself to others.

The Marian counter-example for envy can be seen in the story of the Wedding at Cana. Mary does not snicker or criticize at the social faux pas of running out of wine at a wedding feast, but tells Jesus that the host is in trouble, and then tells the waiters to "do whatever he tells you" (John 2:1-5). May we be as detached from envy, and look with love upon others in their successes and failures.

QUESTIONS FOR UNDERSTANDING

1. Read Isaiah 26:12 and Philippians 2:12-13. Who should receive the glory for every good thing we do? How does Paul understand the way in which we should view our accomplishments in light of our relationship to God?

2. Read 1 Corinthians 12:4-31. How does Paul say that we are to understand our relationship to one another and the relative importance of our contributions?

3. Read Galatians 5:14-26. What is the source of what Paul sees: envy, competition, pride, self-conceit, vying for position and status, factionalism, drunkenness, and other such sins? What is the result of giving in to these sins? What does Paul tell us is the only way to defeat these sins? How do we put that into practice?

4. Read CCC 2538-2540. How does the tenth commandment illuminate the sin of envy in the heart? What does St. John Chrysostom prescribe as the best medicine for killing the sin of envy?

QUESTIONS FOR APPLICATION

1. Have you ever felt resentment over somebody's success or joy over his or her failure? If so, do you still struggle with it, or did you defeat that in your heart? How?

2. Why is envy the daughter of pride and not, say, avarice or gluttony?

3. Dante's penance for the envious is that they have their eyes sewn shut as medieval falconers would sew shut the eyes of their falcons. How is this both a punishment and a medicine for the envious? What does this tell us about the sin of envy?

4. Have you ever had a hero or someone you deeply admired? Who was it and why did you admire him or her so much? If you could meet him or her, what would you say? Can you contrast the admiration you have had for a hero with an experience of envy you have had for a competitor?

5. Can you think of one person in your life who you need to "go out of your way" to praise? Have you ever, like John the Baptist, said of another you were tempted to envy, "He must increase, and I must decrease?" Have you ever had a sense of contentment in knowing where you begin and where you end without having to compare yourself to others?

NOTES:

ANGER & FORGIVENESS

Because hurt is everywhere, anger is everywhere. Scripture tells us "Be angry but do not sin" (Ephesians 4:26). This surprising advice from St. Paul points to the truth about anger: namely, that it is a normal part of human existence (like hunger) and that it is not sinful except when used for the wrong purposes. St. Thomas Aquinas describes the sin of anger as "an unreasonable, irrational, and immoderate desire for vengeance." Given our fallen condition, this is quite common. When somebody hurts us, we don't want mere justice that responds in equal measure to the sin we have suffered. We want overwhelming retaliation that destroys our enemy. This is why, for instance, the law of Moses finds it necessary to prescribe "eye for eye, tooth for tooth, hand for hand, foot for foot, burn for burn, wound for wound, stripe for stripe" (Exodus 21:24-25). It's not because ancient Israelites were barbarians radically different from us. It's because they were barbarians just like us who would, if they could, render an arm and a leg for a foot, a life for an eye, or a life for a wound. The law of Moses was given in order to rein in our thirst to up the ante in the cycle of violence. But it was more than the law of Moses could do to break that cycle. Only Jesus can wash away the sin of the world by letting sin spend itself on him on the cross, and then swallowing it up in his divine mercy.

Dante punishes the angry by inundating them with smoke. When you are in an angry rage, you don't see things correctly, something like being blinded by smoke. Or when you try to talk in anger, you can't get the words out right and it's something like choking in a smoky room. Anger cuts off our ability to listen as well, rendering productive communication impossible.

The lively virtue or antidote to anger is forgiveness, one of the New Testament's most central themes. God is always trying to untie us from these deadly sins that we've wrapped around ourselves, and he's all about unlimited forgiveness. In the Gospel of Matthew (18:21-22), Peter asks how many times he must forgive his brother and Jesus answers, 70x7 times, which means in effect over and over again. Unlimited. Always.

As seen in the Lord's Prayer, there is a clear relationship between God's forgiveness of us and our forgiveness of others. We pray, "Forgive us our trespasses as we forgive those who trespass against us." Someone's inability to forgive is linked to a enlarged sense of the self: "I belong

to me;" "It's my life;" "My dignity has been compromised." Forgiveness cannot be justified on purely humanistic grounds as the concerns of ego or justice will always intervene. Only when we put our forgiveness of others in relationship to God's forgiveness of us will we be able to truly forgive. That's because to forgive, I have to accept that my life is not about me and I exist for God's purposes, which includes being an instrument of his peace.

What does forgiveness look like? It's not simply a movement of the mind or will. It's also not a willful ignorance (i.e., "forgive and forget"). Forgiveness is an active engagement of evil in order to undue it. "Love your enemy" so you can get in the way of and break the cycle of violence. Don't answer in kind, but don't give in to violence either. When you meet fire with fire, you enflame and awaken the blaze. If you meet it with forgiveness, you diffuse the power of evil just as Jesus did on the cross when he took all the sin of the world upon himself, forgave it, and swallowed it up in the divine mercy.

Martin Luther King put this type of forgiveness into practice. He sent African Americans to the all-white lunch counter, and they were arrested. So, he sent more, repeatedly, to wear down the evil of segregation. On a rare occasion, we see someone forgiving a criminal who murdered a loved one. Someone like this knows how to interrupt the horrible rhythm of anger and violence by forgiving and not seeking revenge.

Anger is a legitimate response to injustice. We are right to be angry at injustices as this type of anger is a passion to set things right. A good example is God's anger in Scripture. God burns with a passion to set things right. However, the *deadly* sin of anger is an irrational quest for vengeance. Dr. King did not want to destroy white America, but draw them back into a right relationship with minorities. Legitimate anger is tethered to love. It is an act of willing the good, even if it means loving enemies to draw them into a positive relationship. We sinners tend to cling to our anger and our resentment.

Bishop Barron's offers practical advice to encourage forgiveness:

1. Take a *concrete* step today to heal a broken relationship, such as writing a note or making a phone call. Don't let forgiveness be just a vague abstraction; do something concrete.

2. When you're offended, forgive quickly, and don't brood in your anger. If you hold on to your anger and withhold your forgiveness, the devil has more time to work on you, tempting you to sin.

3. Get in the way of gossip or scapegoating. St. Augustine had a sign over his dinner table: "No one speaks ill of his brother at this table." St. Augustine enforced this as he would ask brothers to leave if they spoke ill of one another.

4. Keep your own sins in mind as this helps you realize that you have been forgiven far more than others have offended you. Really listen and reflect on your sins during the confiteor at Mass ("I confess to almighty God and to you, my brothers and sisters, that I have greatly sinned...") Go to confession. Forgiveness is made palpable through this great sacrament, and it makes you a better forgiver.

Dante's Marian counter-example is when she finds Jesus in temple after three days of looking. Mary's mild response is an antidote to her anger as she says only what is necessary in a positive way. As St. Paul said in his letter to the Ephesians:

> *No foul language should come out of your mouths, but only such as is good for needed edification, that it may impart grace to those who hear. All bitterness, fury, anger, shouting, and reviling must be removed from you, along with all malice. Be kind to one another, compassionate, forgiving one another as God has forgiven you in Christ.*
> *-Ephesians 4:29-32*

Following Mary's example, we should allow God's desire to forgive the world to surge through us.

QUESTIONS FOR UNDERSTANDING

1. Read Mark 3:1-5, John 2:13-17 and CCC 1765. Is anger always a sin? When is anger justified and when is it a sin?

2. Read Matthew 26:50-54 and Luke 22:50-51. How does Jesus confront evil? How does Peter confront evil? What are the differences? According to Bishop Barron, what do the Fathers of the Church see imaged in this incident that teaches us about the difference between the sin of anger and the grace of God?

3. Read Romans 12:17-21. How does this way of confronting evil demonstrate both the power and humility of God? To whom does vengeance belong, and as such, how are we to respond when it seems that vengeance is needed?

4. Read Matthew 6:9-15 and Matthew 18:23-34. What is the condition Jesus puts on the prayer for forgiveness in the Our Father? What is the promise and the warning of that condition? What does the parable of the Unmerciful Servant suggest about the importance of the slights we receive compared with our sins that God has forgiven?

5. Read Colossians 3:12-13. What is the root and basis of our forgiveness of one another? How does St. Paul say we should treat one another because of this root of forgiveness?

QUESTIONS FOR APPLICATION

1. Dante pictures the penitent angry as being inundated with smoke. How is anger like smoke? How can anger cloud our vision? How have you "cleared the air" of anger with somebody through forgiveness?

2. Bishop Barron says that forgiveness involves more than mere thought or a change in attitude, such as "not wishing harm on somebody." Forgiveness requires breaking the cycle of violence by letting evil spend itself and be met with love and mercy. He gives examples of the non-violent resistance of Martin Luther King, Jr. and of Gandhi. Have you ever been in a situation where you or somebody you know turned the other cheek? What was that like? What was the result?

3. Can you think of places in our culture where the forgiveness of sins is rejected as "weak" or wrong? How can we make it clear that forgiveness and mercy are the ultimate examples of the power of God?

4. Is there somebody in your life that you need to forgive? What one positive, concrete step can you take today to confront your sin of anger with the forgiving power of Christ?

SLOTH & ZEAL

When we come to the Cornice of the Slothful, we come to the "dead center" of the entire Divine Comedy, midway up Mount Purgatory and midway through the poem. This place, like the eye of a hurricane, is the fitting spot to discuss sloth, which St. Thomas defined as "sorrow or indifference to spiritual good," and which medieval people called the "noonday devil." Sloth is when a human heart becomes bored with and inert to the things of God. It is not the same thing as mere laziness. "Rather, sloth is identified with avoidance of the difficult, arduous, tedious, laborious goods that our vocations so often demand of us," said Dr. Tom Neal, Professor of Spiritual Theology at Notre Dame Seminary in New Orleans. "The slothful seek the path of least resistance, and so forsake both the small and great heroisms daily life can afford us." A person can be mired in the depths of sloth while filled with energy for video games, TV, career, money, and all the other distractions the world provides, which keep us numb to the voice of God and the desire for holiness.

The Protestant theologian, Karl Barth, thinks sloth is the deadliest sin because the slothful are bored and indifferent with nothing to shake them out of it. Other deadly sins, such as pride, envy, or anger, usually lead to a fall in which you recognize your sin and fervently seek to go back to God. Sloth abounds in our secular society as many are indifferent to spiritual, transcendent things. Absolute, objective truth is no longer accepted culturally, replaced with relativism (i.e., your truth can be different than my truth and we're both right). Even in the U.S. Catholic population, sloth predominates as more than 75% of Catholics don't go to Mass regularly.

St. John of the Cross wrote about the slothful, calling them spiritual "beginners":

> *Beginners also become bored when told to do something unpleasant. Because they look for spiritual gratifications and delights, they are extremely lax in the fortitude and labor perfection demands. Like those who are reared in luxury, they run sadly from everything rough, and they are scandalized by the cross, in which spiritual delights are found. Since they expect to go about in spiritual matters according to the whims and satisfactions of their own will, entering by the narrow way of life, about which Christ speaks, is saddening and repugnant to them.*

Bishop Barron reminds us that the antidote for sloth is zeal for God. This is best kindled by fervent prayer for God to reveal our mission in life, coupled with the vigorous pursuit of the corporal and spiritual works of mercy. Christians are called to be on fire for the Gospel, which is the Good News that Jesus Christ is risen from the dead. We are all made for a definite purpose and each person's purpose revolves around being a conduit of God's love in some particular way.

Dante's punishment for the slothful is that they have to run continually as they hear the line, repeated over and over, "She proceeded in haste" (Luke 1:39). When Mary received her mission at the Annunciation, she knew what she needed to do. The next thing we hear is that "she set out in haste" to visit her cousin Elizabeth. Once you find your mission, get to it right away.

Practical advice from Bishop Barron to guard again sloth includes:

1. Work hard to find and pray to understand your mission. God will respond to your prayer using secondary causes. Pick up the Bible and read it with the urgent question of "What is my mission?"

2. Go to Mass to receive inspiration from Scripture, and spiritual energy from the real presence of Christ in the Eucharist.

3. Perform the corporeal and spiritual works of mercy (CCC 2447) on a regular basis. Most likely, you'll find your mission revealed through these works as it will look like one of them in some way.

QUESTIONS FOR UNDERSTANDING

1. Read Psalm 73. In what ways is the psalmist tempted to be slothful? How does he deal with these temptations, and what does he conclude?

2. Read CCC 2733. What is "presumption," and how does acedia (that is, sloth) work to attack and break down our prayer life? How is this destructive of a relationship with the living God?

3. Read Luke 1:39-45. As they run in Dante's Purgatory, Luke 1:39 is the passage the penitent slothful hear. Why was Mary in haste? Who was she going to see? What does this image show us about our Christian calling?

4. Read CCC 2447. What are the corporal (bodily) and spiritual works of mercy? Why are they important to our spiritual life?

5. Read Matthew 25:31-46. Who does Jesus want to receive the corporal and spiritual works of mercy? Who are those people in your life? Does Jesus see our works of mercy mattering only if we do them for "religious" people?

QUESTIONS FOR APPLICATION

1. People often confuse the sin of sloth with laziness. Bishop Barron points out that frenetic interest in the things of this world can often mask our indifference to the things of the Spirit. Have you ever found yourself wrapped up in extreme busyness? What was that like? What did you do to fight it and make sure it didn't separate you from the things of the Spirit?

2. One aspect of sloth is the tendency to say that truth is subjective. Are there places in your life or in the surrounding culture where relativism and the denial of truth are evident? How can we as believers in God, who is Truth, challenge relativism?"

3. Review the list of corporal and spiritual works of mercy from Q. 4 above. Where do you practice the corporal and spiritual works of mercy in your life? Are there particular works of mercy that you focus on? Why? Are there particular works of mercy you neglect? Why?

4. In John 2:13-21, Jesus' zeal for the house of God led him to drive out the moneychangers from the temple and make clear that the true temple was not a stone building, but the temple of his body. In what ways can you be filled with zeal for the house of God and the Body of Christ, which is the Church?

NOTES:

AVARICE & GENEROSITY

Dante's continuing journey up Mount Purgatory means he is becoming lighter, freer and less burdened by sin. In arriving at the Cornice of the Penitent Avaricious, we are looking at a sin which, while less serious than pride, envy, anger and sloth, is still deadly, as are all the capital sins. It is, after all, avarice that sends the rich man to hell in Jesus' parable of Lazarus and the Rich Man. St. Thomas Aquinas tells us that avarice is the "immoderate or unreasonable desire for riches."

Many popes in the contemporary Church have emphasized that the right to own property and explore entrepreneurial opportunities are good things. Even making a profit is fine. So, what makes wealth unreasonable or immoderate? Sin only enters into the situation when we love these created things more than we love God or our neighbor. The moment we care more about riches than about how to use those riches for the common good is the moment we are opening the door to avarice. This Catholic attitude is grounded in creation – God made everything for common use.

The moment we start recognizing our wealth as a gift from God given to us both for our good and for the good of our neighbor—and begin finding ways to share that wealth with our neighbor—is the day we begin to live generously and imitate God, who became poor for our sake that we might become rich.

Some of the saints and Church leaders have recommended specific approaches when thinking about how to use our wealth:

- St. Ambrose said that if you have two shirts, one belongs to you and the other to the man who has not shirt.

- Pope Leo XIII (founder of modern Catholic social teaching) said, "Once the demands of necessity and propriety have been met in your life, the rest belongs to the poor."

- Cardinal Francis George, when addressing the major benefactors of the Archdiocese of Chicago, underscored Jesus' focus on the poor and said, "The poor need you to draw them out of poverty, and you need the poor to keep you out of Hell."

Avarice prevents you from seeing that your resources were given to you for God's purposes. It also prevents you from seeing and working towards the common good. The Prodigal Son in the parable demands his inheritance, saying "give me my share coming to me." Then he wanders off and squanders the wealth. Dante's penitents are purged of the sin of avarice by being fettered face down on the earth. Because avarice looks no further than the accumulation of wealth or its lavish spending on worldly pleasure, the punishment fits the sin: penitents must look only at the earth upon which they wasted their wealth.

In a materialistic culture, those seeking to grow spiritually must search their hearts honestly and frequently to uncover any tendency to be greedy. Is money playing too great a role in my life? How much time do I spend worrying about it? Do I often compare my wealth to others? How painful is it when I have to give money away?

The lively virtue or antidote to avarice is generosity. The Trinity is a community of divine generosity. God is generous love. The Father loves the Son, and the Son loves him back. The Holy Spirit is the result or outpouring of their love. All lively virtues spring from love and are attempts to imitate God.

Dante's Marian counter-example is the fact that Mary gives birth to the King of kings in poverty, while Caesar Augustus, the reigning Roman king, lives in wealthy splendor.

Bishop Barron recommends a few steps to take to cultivate generosity:

1. Give away your goods and money on a regular basis.

2. Clean out your closet and give away something *you like* each month.

3. When shopping for larger ticket items, find the one you want and can afford, and then buy the next one down (i.e., lower in price), and give the dollar difference to the poor.

4. Place a poor box next to your door, and put something in it every time you leave the house.

5. Factor the common good into every one of your economic decisions. Review your checkbook to see how well you are serving the common good.

QUESTIONS FOR UNDERSTANDING

1. Read Matthew 6:19-34 and 1 Timothy 6:6-10. What is the attitude we are to take toward the wealth of this world? What can happen if we relentlessly pursue wealth, "longing to be rich"? What are "treasures in heaven"?

2. Read Luke 16:19-31. How much importance does Jesus place on generosity to the poor?

3. Read CCC 1906-1909. What is meant by the "common good"? What is our personal responsibility for contributing to the common good?

4. Read 2 Corinthians 8:1-15. How does Paul urge the Corinthians to be generous? How does he preserve their freedom and yet call them to give? In verse 15, he cites the story of the manna in the wilderness in Exodus 16. How does this picture of the common good relate to our own use of riches today?

QUESTIONS FOR APPLICATION

1. Avarice is often thought of as a sin of the rich and, to be sure, many rich people are afflicted with this temptation. However, a poor person can also be obsessed with money (and with envy of the rich). Have you ever struggled with an inordinate desire for riches? How does our culture encourage the love of money? How can you overcome this temptation?

2. Pope Leo XIII taught us that once the demands of necessity and propriety have been met, the rest of our wealth belongs to the poor. What is your honest reaction to that? Reflect on the "demands of necessity and propriety" in your own circumstances and whether you should be giving more away.

3. Have you ever been poor yourself and found it necessary to rely on the help of others to get by? What was that like? Did you feel gratitude? Shame? Determination to change your circumstances? Were you able to share with others in some way even when you had little?

4. Jesus says of the poor widow who put two tiny copper coins in the temple treasury that she gave more than all those who had contributed out of their excess. Have you or somebody you know ever given sacrificially? Describe the situation and comment on the outcome of that gift, both to the receiver and to the giver.

5. Dante's penitents are purged of the sin of avarice by being fettered face down on the earth. Because avarice looks no further than the accumulation of wealth or its lavish spending on worldly pleasure, the punishment fits the sin: penitents must look only at the earth upon which they wasted their wealth. Have you ever had a time when you realized that you could never get enough of what you thought you wanted? If so, how did this realization affect your priorities?

NOTES:

GLUTTONY & ASCETICISM

As we continue climbing Mount Purgatory, we become freer of the heavier sins and begin to encounter the lighter ones. This does not make them less deadly, of course, but it does mean that these sins involve "less grave" perversions of the good. Pride, envy and anger are *perverted* love that delight in harm to others. Sloth is *defective* love that fails to take an interest in the things of God. At the top of Dante's mountain, gluttony and lust involve an *excess* of love for sensual pleasure — food, drink, or sex — over the love of God. These two are lighter sins because the glutton and the lustful at least love something. But they remain deadly because those loves take priority over the love of God and neighbor.

We live in a culture of gluttony. Our culture makes it extremely easy to believe that "we deserve a break today," and that we should continually indulge our appetites (the appetite for food being only one of the many). Our faith does not call us to reject food and drink as bad things, but only to use them within reason and with respect for the common good, making sure to prioritize loving God and others.

The psychiatrist and psychoanalyst, Karl Jung, said psychological problems are usually spiritual problems. Gluttony is a physiological and psychological problem for sure, but also a spiritual one as gluttons try to satisfy their deep hunger for God in the wrong way. St. Augustine said that God has made us for himself "so our hearts are restless until we rest in thee." We often substitute finite goods for the infinite and try to fill up our infinite hunger with created things. They don't satisfy, so we panic and think we need more and more of them, often leading to addiction.

Catholics are not puritans who eschew all sensual pleasures. Catholics enjoy sensual pleasures (food, drink and sex) as gifts from God. However, sensual pleasures need to be disciplined to be rightly ordered. Thomas Merton once remarked that our hunger for food, drink, shelter, and sex are like children – insistently demanding immediate satisfaction. These desires can dominate the soul very quickly, if we let them. If we indulge them, they will take over.

Right after Jesus's baptism, he was "led by the Spirit into the desert to be tempted by the devil" (Matt 4:1). Why would God the Father want anyone to go into the desert? We all must discipline our insistent desires to allow greater goods to emerge. The desert provides a "stripping away" so that the most important, fundamental things will appear. In the desert, there are no distractions, no secondary matters, no diversions, so you can then discover strengths and weaknesses that you don't even know you have and grow closer to God.

After fasting for 40 days and 40 nights, Jesus was hungry. The devil's first temptation was to suggest that Jesus turn the desert stones into loaves of bread. This symbolizes turning sensual pleasure into the dominant force in your life. There's nothing wrong with food or bread. But there is a problem with making food, drink or any sensual pleasure the most basic good of your life. Prioritizing the hedonistic adage to "eat, drink and be merry" will make satisfaction of bodily desires the center of your life. If you make bodily desires predominant, then the deeper and more abiding spiritual hungers never surface.

The deeper and more abiding hunger is our hunger for God. Our most basic good comes in following the will and purposes of God. Jesus replied to the devil's first temptation by quoting Scripture (Deuteronomy): "One does not live by bread alone, but by every word that comes forth from the mouth of God" (Matt 4:4). Once we are clear on what is the most basic good, we will know how to rightly order sensual pleasures.

The antidote to gluttony is asceticism. Asceticism creates a "desert environment" within us that helps discipline our lower nature to allow the higher desires to emerge. If we don't discipline our hunger for sensual pleasures, they will come to dominate our lives. It's interesting that most of us accept the need to practice asceticism or discipline to improve our physical health, but we often don't embrace it to improve our spiritual health. Fasting, an ancient and powerful spiritual practice, offers a well-suited antidote for gluttony. We fast so the deeper hunger for God will become evident. Without some denial of sensual pleasure, we might never realize that we even have a hunger for God.

Bishop Barron's practical advice to avoid gluttony includes:

1. A serious fast from a food or drink you love dearly.

2. Skip a meal or a night out and spend time in prayer. This reminds us to downplay our hunger for food and drink, and replace it with a hunger and thirst for God.

3. Go away from table feeling hungry.

4. Don't fast simply as self-punishment. As you fast, feel that hunger, and then treat it as a kind of sacrament of your higher-order hunger for the Divine. Make the connection in your prayer, such as saying "Lord, I know this is symbolic of my hunger and thirst for you."

Dante's punishment for gluttons is that they are made to say, "O Lord, open my lips and my mouth to declare your praise." Instead of opening their lips to eat, they open them to pray one of the Psalms.

As you ponder the sin of gluttony and its lively virtue, asceticism, pay attention to ways in which you may be tempted toward excessive love of food and drink. Also, consider models you may have seen of people with a balanced and moderate approach to their appetites. Ask God for the grace to acquire self-discipline so that you can have the happiness you truly desire.

QUESTIONS FOR UNDERSTANDING

1. Read Genesis 3 and Matthew 4:1-4. What is the devil trying to get Jesus to do? How does this parallel Satan's temptation of Adam and Eve? How does Jesus answer the Tempter? How can you apply the passage Jesus cites from Deuteronomy 8:3 to your life?

2. Read Matthew 11:16-19. What do Jesus' enemies accuse him of? What does this suggest about Jesus' attitude toward the goodness of food and drink? What does it suggest about the attitudes of his enemies?

3. Read Matthew 6:16-21. What is to be our attitude as we fast? How does this relate to Bishop Barron's point that gluttony is the attempt to gain happiness from sources that can't give it to us? How do fasting and prayer directly challenge this disordered desire?

4. Read Isaiah 58. How does God tell Israel to make a fast pleasing to him? What does God promise us when we fast in the spirit he desires?

QUESTIONS FOR APPLICATION

1. Do you or somebody you know struggle with enslavement to excessive love of food and/or drink? Do you know people with the opposite problem: a fear of eating? How do these disordered appetites push the love of God and neighbor out of the center of our lives?

2. There's an expression: "You can never get enough of what you don't really want." Have you ever experienced using food as a way of trying to fill an inner emptiness that God is meant to fill? Did you overcome it? How?

3. Bishop Barron compares asceticism to using a Stairmaster so that you can become healthier. In the spiritual life, we are likewise called to asceticism to discipline our appetites and become spiritually healthier by opening our lives to God. Have you ever tried an ascetic practice such as fasting? What were the benefits you gained?

4. Have you ever tried making a deliberate sacrifice of something you love, not out of an attempt to "diet" but as an offering to God and for his Church? What did you do and what happened when you did?

NOTES:

LUST & CHASTITY

C.S. Lewis once remarked that he was a converted pagan living in a country of apostate Puritans. He was speaking of Britain, but much the same could be said of American culture. Our apostate Puritan culture has long taught us to believe that the very worst sin in the world is lust. But Dante regards lust as the lightest and least serious of the deadly sins. It is, like gluttony, an excess of love for *something* rather than the choice to reject love. What it is not, however, is an excess of love for another person, despite the fact that it involves sex. That's the main problem with it: lust is the sin of treating another person as an object or as a means to an end. Lewis remarks that the lustful man does not "want a woman." He wants an experience for which the woman happens to be the necessary apparatus. In short, lust treats people like things and insults the love and dignity they are due as human beings.

While Dante sees lust as the lightest of the deadly sins, we see lust as the *worst* sin. This may be caused by a Puritan influence, which teaches that spirit is good and matter is evil or fallen. So to a Puritan, the whole purpose of life is to escape from matter, especially from sexuality, which so ties us to the material realm. But authentic Biblical Christianity is not puritanical. The Creator God described in the book of Genesis made the entire panoply of things physical — planets, stars, the moon and sun, animals, fish and found all of it good, even very good. Accordingly, there is nothing perverse or morally questionable about bodies, sex, sexual longing or the sexual act. In fact, it's just the contrary. When, in the Gospel of Mark, Jesus himself is asked about marriage and sexuality, he hearkens back to the book of Genesis and the story of creation: "At the beginning of creation God made them male and female; for this reason a man shall leave his father and mother and the two shall become as one. They are no longer two but one flesh" (Mk. 10:6-8). That last sentence is, dare I say it, inescapably "sexy." Jesus most certainly was no Puritan.

So, given this stress on the goodness of sex and sexual pleasure, what separates the Christian view from, say, the "Playboy" philosophy? The simple answer is that, for Biblical people, sexuality must be placed in the wider framework of love, which is to will the good of the other. It is fundamental to Catholic spirituality and morality that everything in life must be drawn magnetically toward love, must be conditioned and transfigured by love. The goodness of sexual

desire is designed, by its very nature, to become ingredient in a program of self-forgetting love and hence to become something rare and life enhancing. If you want to see what happens when this principle is ignored, take a long hard look at the hookup culture prevalent among many young — and not so young — people today. Sex as mere recreation, as contact sport, as a source only of superficial pleasure has produced armies of the desperately sad and anxious, many who have no idea that it is precisely their errant sexuality that has produced such deleterious effects in them. When sexual pleasure is drawn out of itself by the magnetic attraction of love, it is rescued from self-preoccupation and lust.

The heart of the moral life was summarized by Emmanuel Kant when he said, "never treat another human being as a means, but only as an end." This principle was central to St. John Paul II's writing on sexual ethics. Receiving much criticism, St. John Paul II wrote that lust can happen in marriage because even spouses can treat each other in an objectifying way. The lustful take the sexual drive within them, which is meant to be a means of allowing the divine life to flow through them, and misuse it for their own, self-satisfying purposes.

One of the most egregious examples of lust is pornography, which is a multi-billion enterprise that has exploded online. There are approximately 107 million visitors to adult websites each month in the U.S., and the average age of first exposure to porn among boys is 11 (*Time Magazine*, April 11, 2016). The Catholic Church—and indeed all of decent society until about forty years ago—sees pornography as, first and foremost, an ethical violation, a deep distortion of human sexuality, an unconscionable objectification of persons who should never be treated as anything less than subjects. That this ethical distortion results in myriad problems, both physical and psychological, goes without saying, but the Catholic conviction is that those secondary consequences will not be adequately addressed unless the underlying issue of sex divorced from love is tackled.

The lively virtue or antidote to lust is chastity, meaning "sexual uprightness." Chastity is a profound respect for the otherness of the other, a refusal to turn the other into an object. Unless you can turn to someone you love and say, "I don't need you," you can't authentically love that person. Love as "willing the good of the other" is very different than a love that just satisfies your own needs. To love someone is to will their own good, regardless of your own desires.

Practical advice from Bishop Barron to avoid lust:

1. If you are using pornography or are involved in some manipulative, objectifying sexual relationship, stop it immediately.

2. Get help if you are addicted to sex in any way.

3. Examine the quality of your relationships, especially the most intimate ones. To what degree is "need" playing a dominant role? Do you really unselfishly "will the good" of the one you love?

Dante's Marian counter-example is from the Annunciation. Upon learning she is about to conceive, Mary asks, "How can this be, since I have no relations with a man?" (Luke 1:34). Her response represents her purity and chastity as she has always been unwilling to allow her sexual desire to objectify another.

After being purified from lust by passing through fire, Dante is ready to fly to Paradise from the top of Mount Purgatory. God wants all of us to be light and free, ready to fly, but sin, often an outgrowth of fear, keeps us captive. We are like Lazarus in the tomb, dead in our sins. But Jesus says, "Come out. Untie him and let him go" (John 11:43-44). God is about the business of liberation and is loving you right now into existence. So relax, find your mission, and let God's love flow through you to all the world.

QUESTIONS FOR UNDERSTANDING

1. Read Matthew 5:27-30. Where does Jesus see lust beginning? Jesus uses hyperbole to point out the need for radical repentance from the sin of lust. Why is such drastic action demanded? What does this suggest about the addictive nature of lust?

2. St. John Paul II warned that people can commit the sin of lust even *within* marriage. What do you think he meant?

3. Read 1 Corinthians 6:12-20. God has made you so that his love can surge through you and enable you to love others for their own sake and not for your use and exploitation. Given that, why does Paul find lust so grave a sin against Christ?

4. Read 1 John 2:15-17. What does John mean by "lust"? How does it relate to pride? What does John say about this world and its relationship to lust?

5. Read CCC 2392-2400. What is chastity? Who is the model of chastity? What is the difference between chastity and celibacy?

QUESTIONS FOR APPLICATION

1. What are some of the temptations in our culture toward lust? What are some ways we can arm ourselves against these temptations?

2. Have you ever had an experience of falling in love? How was it different from mere lust?

3. People talk about pornography as a "victimless crime." Do you agree with this statement? Why or why not?

4. Dante's penitent lustful must pass through fire to be cleansed of this sin. How is this again a punishment that fits the sin? What in your life needs to be burned up in order to free you from the sin of lust?

5. Do you know some model—whether in Scripture, among the saints, or in your life—of the practice of joyful chastity? What concrete step could you take today to imitate that?

BIOGRAPHICAL INFORMATION

BISHOP ROBERT BARRON

Bishop Robert Barron is the founder of Word on Fire Catholic Ministries and the host of *CATHOLICISM*, a groundbreaking, award-winning documentary about the Catholic Faith. In July 2015, Pope Francis appointed him auxiliary bishop of the Archdiocese of Los Angeles. He previously served as the Rector-President of Mundelein Seminary/University of St. Mary of the Lake from 2012 until 2015.

Bishop Barron's website, *WordOnFire.org*, reaches millions of people each year. The site hosts daily blog posts, weekly articles and video commentaries, and an extensive audio archive of homilies. Bishop Barron's homilies are heard by tens of thousands of visitors each week. His regular YouTube videos have been viewed millions of times, and thousands of people receive his daily email reflections through *DailyCatholicGospel.com*.

EWTN (The Eternal Word Television Network) and CatholicTV broadcast Bishop Barron's videos and documentaries to a worldwide audience of over 150 million people. His weekly Word on Fire radio program has been broadcast in Chicago (WGN) and throughout the country (Relevant Radio - 950 AM Chicago) to over 30 million listeners.

Bishop Barron is a #1 Amazon bestselling author and has published twelve books and hundreds of essays and articles on theology and the spiritual life. He works with NBC News in New York as an on-air contributor and analyst. He is also a frequent commentator for the *Chicago Tribune, FOX News, CNN, EWTN, Our Sunday Visitor,* the *Catholic Herald* in London, and *Catholic News Agency*.

Bishop Barron's pioneering work in evangelizing through the new media led Francis Cardinal George to describe him as "one of the Church's best messengers." He has keynoted many conferences and events all over the world, including the opening keynote talk at the 2015 World Meeting of Families. He was appointed to the theological faculty of Mundelein Seminary in 1992, and has also served as a visiting professor at the University of Notre Dame and at the Pontifical University of St. Thomas Aquinas. He was twice scholar in residence at the Pontifical North American College at the Vatican. Ordained in 1986 in the Archdiocese of Chicago, Bishop Barron received a Master's Degree in Philosophy from the Catholic University of America in 1982 and a doctorate in Sacred Theology from the Institut Catholique de Paris in 1992.

MARK P. SHEA

Mark P. Shea is a popular Catholic writer and speaker. Mark was raised as an agnostic, became a non-denominational Evangelical in 1979, and entered the Catholic Church in 1987.

Mark's most recent work is *Mary, Mother of the Son* (Marytown). He contributes articles to many periodicals, including his popular column "Connecting the Dots" for the *National Catholic Register* and his daily blog on Patheos.com. He is also a frequent blogger at *Catholic and Enjoying It!* and at the *Register*. Mark is known nationally for his one minute "Words of Encouragement" on Catholic radio and he has also appeared numerous times on television. In addition, Mark is an internationally known speaker on various issues in Catholic faith and life.

Mark lives in Washington State with his wife, Janet, and their four sons.